EXPLORING BIOLOGY

PLANT & ANIMAL BIOLOGY

by
Tom Jackson

Minneapolis, Minnesota

Credits

Cover and title page, © Dmitry/Adobe Stock, and © Ortis/Adobe Stock; 3 © Anusorn Nakdee/Shutterstock; 4, © VW Pics/Getty Images; 4–5, © Peter-Hg/Shutterstock; 5, © gstraub/Shutterstock; 6M, © Hanahstocks/Shutterstock; 6B, © Public Domain/Wikimedia Commons; 6–7, © Ivanova Ksenia/Shutterstock; 7, © Kuttelvaserova Stuchelova/Shutterstock; 8T, © Sakurra/Shutterstock; 8B, © SP-Photo/Shutterstock; 8–9, © Yusev/Shutterstock; 9T, © Public Domain/Wikimedia Commons; 9B, © Carolina K. Smith MD/Shutterstock; 10M, © Steve Gschmeissner/Science Photo Library; 10B, © Mohammed/Adobe Stock; 10–11, © Mazur Travel/Shutterstock; 11T, © Public Domain/Wikimedia Commons; 12M, © BlueRingMedia/Shutterstock; 12B, © INTERFOTO/Alamy Stock Photo; 12–13, © Midori Photography/Shutterstock; 13T, © Designua/Shutterstock; 14T, © Sakurra/Shutterstock; 14B, © Ldarin/Shutterstock; 14–15, © Golden Family Foto/Shutterstock; 15B, © Public Domain/Wikimedia Commons; 16M, © Sorokin Evgenii/Shutterstock; 16B, © Rhoenbergfoto/Shutterstock; 16–17, © hessianmercenary/Shutterstock; 17T, © Bearport Publishing; 18T, © Wonderly Imaging/Shutterstock; 18B, © firatturgut/Shutterstock; 18–19, © WaterFrame/Alamy Stock Photo; 19, © Atlaspix/Alamy Stock Photo; 20T, © Focused Adventures/Shutterstock; 20–21, © Monkey Business Images/Shutterstock; 21T, © Public Domain/Wikimedia Commons; 21B, © Choksawatdikorn/Shutterstock; 22T, © Vojce/Shutterstock; 22B, © Public Domain/Wikimedia Commons; 22–23, © blue-sea.cz/Shutterstock; 23T, © Marko Blagoevic/Shutterstock; 24T, © mar_chm1982/Shutterstock; 24B, © Hugh Lansdown/Shutterstock; 24–25, © Prathankarnpap/Shutterstock; 25B, © Bearport Publishing; 26T, © DedeDian/Shutterstock; 26B, © Public Domain/Wikimedia Commons; 26–27, © Norjipin Saidi/Shutterstock; 27T, © Tennessee Witney/Shutterstock; 28TR, © moosehenderson/Shutterstock; 28ML, © Epidavros/Shutterstock; 28B, © Universal Images Group North America LLC/Alamy Stock Photo; 28–29, © J. Esteban Berrio/Shutterstock; 29B, © Everett Collection/Shutterstock; 30B, © Paul Vinten/Shutterstock; 30–31, © Nature Picture Libray/Alamy Stock Photo; 31T, © idiz/Shutterstock; 31B, © lev radin/Shutterstock; 32T, © Jacques Sztuke/Shutterstock; 32B, © Oasishifi/Shutterstock; 32–33, © Sergey Uryadnikov/Shutterstock; 33B, © Public Domain/Wikimedia Commons; 34T, © kooanan007/Shutterstock; 34B, © Dave Hansche/Shutterstock; 34–35, © Kurit afshen/Shutterstock; 35T, © Nature Picture Library/Alamy Stock Photo; 36M, © Peter-Hg/Shutterstock; 36B, © Public Domain/Wikimedia Commons; 36–37, © Janelle Lugge/Shutterstock; 37T, © MSMondadori/Shutterstock; 38T, © StevenWhitcherPhotography/Shutterstock; 38B, © A.Sych/Shutterstock; 38–39, © Antje Schulte - Aphid World/Alamy Stock Photo; 39T, © olga gl/Shutterstock; 40T, © beejung/Shutterstock; 40B, © Rudmer Zwerver/Shutterstock; 40–41, © Ken Kiefer/Shutterstock; 41T, © Public Domain/Wikimedia Commons; 41M, © Beverly Speed/Shutterstock; 42, © WESTOCK PRODUCTIONS/Shutterstock; 42–43, © teptong/iStock; 44B, © Midori Photography/Shutterstock; 45T, © Norjipin Saidi/Shutterstock; 45B, © Ken Kiefer/Shutterstock; 47, © J. Esteban Berrio/Shutterstock.

Bearport Publishing Company Product Development Team

Publisher: Jen Jenson; Director of Product Development: Spencer Brinker; Editorial Director: Allison Juda; Editor: Cole Nelson; Editor: Tiana Tran; Production Editor: Naomi Reich; Art Director: Kim Jones; Designer: Kayla Eggert; Designer: Steve Scheluchin; Production Specialist: Owen Hamlin

Statement on Usage of Generative Artificial Intelligence

Bearport Publishing remains committed to publishing high-quality nonfiction books. Therefore, we restrict the use of generative AI to ensure accuracy of all text and visual components pertaining to a book's subject. See BearportPublishing.com for details.

Library of Congress Cataloging-in-Publication Data is available at www.loc.gov or upon request from the publisher.

ISBN: 979-8-89577-495-3 (hardcover)
ISBN: 979-8-89577-537-0 (paperback)
ISBN: 979-8-89577-503-5 (ebook)

© 2026 Arcturus Holdings Limited.
This edition is published by arrangement with Arcturus Publishing Limited.

North American adaptations © 2026 Bearport Publishing Company. All rights reserved. No part of this publication may be reproduced in whole or in part, stored in any retrieval system, or transmitted in any form or by any means, electronic, mechanical, photocopying, recording, or otherwise, without written permission from the publisher. Bearport Publishing is a division of FlutterBee Education Group.

For more information, write to Bearport Publishing, 3500 American Blvd W, Suite 150, Bloomington, MN 55431.

Contents

The Plantae and Animalia Kingdoms 4

Plants. 6

Plant Cells 8

Plant Bodies 10

Plant Reproduction 12

Photosynthesis and Respiration 14

Plants in Extreme Habitats. 16

Animalia. 18

Animal Cells. 20

Simple Invertebrates. 22

Arthropods. 24

Lower Vertebrates 26

Birds. 28

Mammals 30

Social Groups. 32

Animal Bodies 34

Animal Locomotion 36

Animal Reproduction 38

Other Senses 40

More to Explore 42

Review and Reflect 44

Glossary. 46

Read More 47

Learn More Online. 47

Index 48

The Plantae and Animalia Kingdoms

All living things on Earth are split into six different biological kingdoms. Together, the Plantae and Animalia kingdoms account for more than nine million species worldwide—with many more yet to be discovered. Within these kingdoms, there is a vast and diverse variety of species. They come in different shapes and sizes. Many have characteristics that they share and some that are unique to that species specifically.

Common Ancestor

Scientists believe that all plant and animal species share a single common ancestor. This cell from around four billion years ago is often referred to as the last universal common ancestor. Scientists theorize that this shared ancestor lived hidden away in deep-sea vents on the ocean floor, where it made its own food and survived without air.

Eukaryotes

Eukaryotes are living things made of cells that have a nucleus. They can range in size from as small as a microscopic single-celled organism to as large as a blue whale. Eukaryotes can be either unicellular or multicellular. Bacteria and yeast are both examples of unicellular eukaryotes. Palm trees, toucans, and many other plants and animals are multicellular.

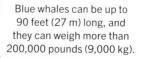

Blue whales can be up to 90 feet (27 m) long, and they can weigh more than 200,000 pounds (9,000 kg).

4

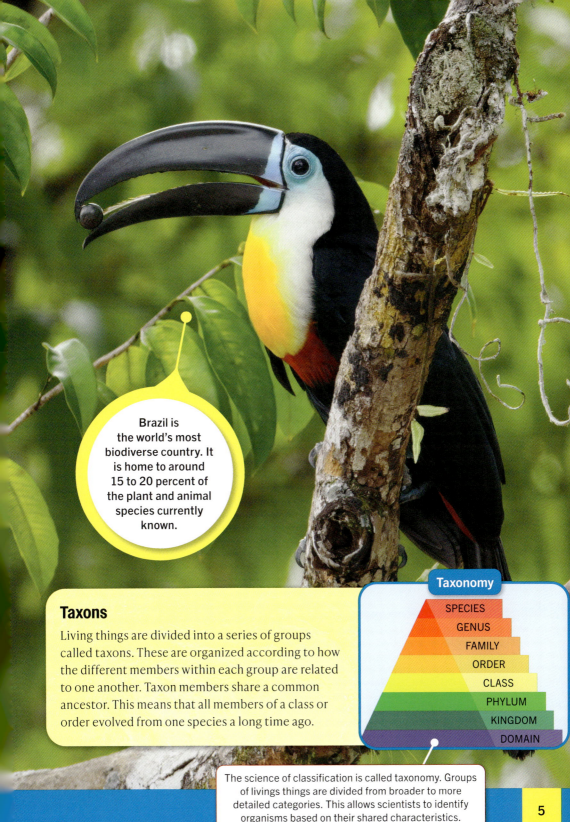

Brazil is the world's most biodiverse country. It is home to around 15 to 20 percent of the plant and animal species currently known.

Taxons

Living things are divided into a series of groups called taxons. These are organized according to how the different members within each group are related to one another. Taxon members share a common ancestor. This means that all members of a class or order evolved from one species a long time ago.

Taxonomy

SPECIES
GENUS
FAMILY
ORDER
CLASS
PHYLUM
KINGDOM
DOMAIN

The science of classification is called taxonomy. Groups of livings things are divided from broader to more detailed categories. This allows scientists to identify organisms based on their shared characteristics.

5

Plants

There are around a quarter of a million species of plants that make up the kingdom Plantae, with members ranging from tiny mosses to towering trees. Plants power their bodies through photosynthesis—a process that uses the energy in sunlight to make sugar from water and carbon dioxide. Aside from the coldest and driest habitats, plants are found in all parts of the world.

> The giant sequoia is one of the largest and longest-living organisms on Earth. It grows to about 280 ft. (85 m) tall and lives for more than 3,000 years!

Internal Vessels

Moss is one of the simplest kinds of plants. It grows over surfaces, and its flat body has no distinct roots, stem, or leaves. Mosses are nonvascular plants, which means they don't have a channel to transport water or nutrients. Vascular plants, such as ferns, conifers, and flowering plants, have vessels that can transport water and sugar around them. This makes their bodies stiff enough to grow up toward the light.

The giant sequoia is a conifer. It uses cones to breed and make seeds. Most plants grow flowers, not cones, for this purpose.

Moss is mostly green because it is full of a green chemical called chlorophyll that absorbs red and blue sunlight in order to make food.

HALL OF FAME

Janaki Ammal
1897–1984

Janaki Ammal was one of the first women to study botany. She bred new kinds of crops that would grow better in her home country, India. This allowed the country to produce more of its own food. At the same time, Ammal also campaigned to keep India's habitats as natural as possible.

Seaweed

Seaweeds are plants that live in the oceans. They are not usually included in the Plantae kingdom. Instead, seaweeds are types of algae that grow into large, multicellular bodies. They photosynthesize and need sunlight to survive as land plants do, and so they grow mostly in shallow, sunlit water. Seaweeds have no roots but are anchored to the seabed. Instead of leaves, they have fronds that float in the water.

When the tide goes out, seaweeds are exposed to the air. Many seaweeds cover their fronds in waterproof slime to stay moist.

Trees usually grow above smaller plants to collect more sunlight. They strengthen their bodies with wood to grow tall.

DID YOU KNOW? Plants make up 80 percent of all the living material on Earth! In total, that is 496 billion tons (450 billion t).

Plant Cells

Plants have a distinctive cell structure that sets them apart from other kingdoms of life. The most obvious feature is the cell wall that surrounds the cell's outer membrane and provides structural support. Additionally, the cells in the green parts of a plant have chloroplasts that are used for photosynthesis.

Internal Structures

All cells share some basic features. They are filled with a watery liquid called cytoplasm, which is contained inside an enveloping cell membrane. The cells of complex life, such as plants, have a nucleus where the deoxyribonucleic acid (DNA) is stored. Plant cells typically have a large vacuole. This is a bag used to store water, salts, and sugars.

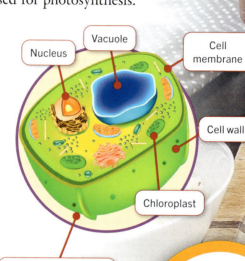

Nucleus · Vacuole · Cell membrane · Cell wall · Chloroplast

The cell wall of one plant cell is glued to its neighbors, creating strong plant bodies.

This wooden cutting board is composed of dead plant cells made of cellulose walls filled with a hard polymer called lignin.

Hay is almost pure cellulose. Farm animals have stomach bacteria that can digest this dried grass stalk.

Tough Cell Wall

The plant cell wall is made from a carbohydrate called cellulose. This is a polymer, or chainlike chemical, that is made from smaller glucose molecules joined together. The structure of cellulose makes it a very sturdy substance, which strengthens plant bodies enough to stand upright. Cellulose is left behind even after all the other parts of the cells have rotted away.

HALL OF FAME

Robert Hooke
1635–1703
Robert Hooke was one of the first scientists to use a microscope. In 1665, he used the tool to study a thin piece of cork from the bark of a cork oak tree. Hooke found that it was made from many tiny compartments. He thought they looked like the cramped living quarters in monasteries—rooms called cells. That term has been used ever since.

An onion is a plant body part called a bulb. During winter, this body part allows a plant to store food underground so that it can sprout again in spring.

The individual cells of a thin layer of onion skin are easy to see under a microscope. These have been dyed so the starch stored in the cells shows up as purple.

DID YOU KNOW? Plant cells are often rectangular in shape. They are usually between 0.0004 and 0.004 inches (0.01 and 0.1 mm) long.

Plant Bodies

Plants range in size from the tallest tree to the tiniest daisy, but they follow the same basic body plan. The lower part is made of roots that extend into the soil. In the middle of the plant, there is a stem that often divides into branches before sprouting leaves on the upper part of the plant.

> The older xylem tubes in thicker stems are filled with a hard material to make wood. Tree trunks are very strong, so these plants can grow to heights of more than 330 ft. (100 m).

Transportation Vessels

Most plants have an internal network of vessels that run up the stem between the roots and leaves. In plants, xylem is a type of tissue that carries water and dissolved nutrients and salts. It is made from dead cells with open ends, which form stiff tubes that also provide structural support to the plant. Phloem tissue moves sugars—the plant's energy source—from the leaves where they are made to the rest of the plant.

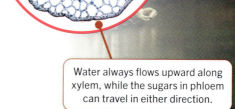

Water always flows upward along xylem, while the sugars in phloem can travel in either direction.

The stomata are mostly on the underside of the leaf. This prevents water from evaporating in strong sunlight.

Leaf Anatomy

A leaf is basically a plant's solar panel, stretched out thin and flat to help it catch as much light as possible. Light enters through the top, where the cells are packed with chloroplasts to capture its energy. The water needed for photosynthesis is provided by vessels in the leaf's central vein. Carbon dioxide from the air enters gas spaces in the lower part of the leaf through pores called stomata.

HALL OF FAME

Agnes Arber
1879–1960

Agnes Arber became interested in botany while still at school. She later began a career as a full-time scientist and started to publish books on plants. These works were groundbreaking in the way they described plant bodies scientifically. Arber was an expert in conifers and grasses.

Roots need a supply of air and water. These mangrove trees have sturdy woody roots above the water, so they can get air.

Bark is not the same as wood. It has waxy chemicals to make it waterproof, and there are often smelly oils and resins that keep insects and other invaders away.

DID YOU KNOW? Pando is a forest in Utah with about 40,000 aspen trees that are all connected underground, making it the world's largest plant.

Plant Reproduction

The two main types of plants that grow on land—flowering plants and conifers—reproduce by making seeds. Seeds are created when pollen grains carrying male sex cells fuse with female ovules, which hold egg cells. During this process, known as pollination, pollen is moved from plant to plant by the wind, water, or animals.

> Flowers use bright colors and powerful odors to attract insects and other animals. The animals come to eat a sweet liquid produced by the flower called nectar.

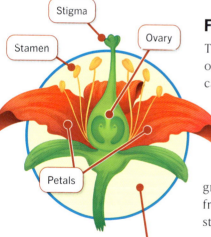

Flowers

The flower is a plant's sexual organ. Pollen is produced on tall stalks called stamens, while the ovules are held in the ovary in the center of the flower. Wind-pollinated flowers produce dry, dustlike pollen that blows away easily. Flowers that rely on animals, such as insects, for pollination create sticky grains that cling to animal bodies. Pollen from another flower sticks to the central stigma and burrows into the ovary.

> After pollination, the ovary develops seeds, and the surrounding region grows into a fruit. The fruit is designed to spread the seeds so new plants can grow.

HALL OF FAME

Karl von Frisch
1886–1982

Honeybees are famous for dancing. The insects do this to communicate with others about the best locations for good foraging. Karl von Frisch discovered the honeybee dance and translated its meaning. In 1973, he won the Nobel Prize for this important breakthrough.

Germination

Germination is the process by which a seed sprouts into a new plant. This is stimulated by temperature, water levels, and the length of daylight. Under the right conditions, a shoot will emerge from the seed, growing toward the light and away from gravity. The seed contains one or two embryonic leaves called cotyledons. These leaves contain a store of nutrients that fuel growth until the first true leaves can form and photosynthesize.

Leaves

Cotyledon

Stem

Seed   Root

The radicle is the plant's first root. It does the opposite of the stem. The radicle grows toward the pull of gravity and away from light.

Honeybees are one of the most important pollinators. They carry nectar and pollen back to the nest. The nectar and pollen are the raw ingredients for making honey, the bees' main food.

Animals carry pollen grains from flower to flower, where they can be used in reproduction. Some animals eat pollen as well, but there is plenty to spare.

DID YOU KNOW? The smallest pollen is made by the forget-me-not flower. It is about 6 microns (0.006 mm) long, which is almost the same size as a bacterium.

13

Photosynthesis and Respiration

All life on Earth requires a source of energy to power its metabolism, or life processes. This energy is delivered through the processes of photosynthesis and respiration. Photosynthesis is used by plants to convert the energy in sunlight into sugar fuels. Animals use respiration to release the energy in sugars for metabolism.

Chloroplasts

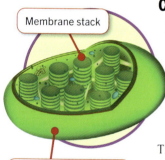

Membrane stack

Chlorophyll is bonded to stacks of membranes inside the chloroplast. This molecule looks green because it absorbs red and blue light but reflects back green light waves.

Photosynthesis occurs in plant cells inside green capsules called chloroplasts. They are green because they contain the pigment chlorophyll. When sunlight hits chlorophyll, some of its energy is absorbed. This energy is used to combine carbon dioxide gas from the air and water to create a simple sugar called glucose. The process produces oxygen as a waste product, which is given out by the plant. The same process of photosynthesis occurs in some bacteria, but bacteria do not use chloroplasts to hold chlorophyll.

Mitochondria

Respiration is the reverse of photosynthesis. It is when oxygen reacts with glucose to release energy as it breaks up into carbon dioxide and water. In complex life, respiration happens inside cell structures called mitochondria. The glucose and oxygen react in several small steps so energy is released slowly. The carbon dioxide produced by respiration must be removed from animal bodies, although plants can use it again for photosynthesis.

Mitochondria are surrounded by two membranes. Respiration happens close to the inner one, which is highly folded to increase its area.

Plants are autotrophs. They use photosynthesis to create their own food supply. This food is used in respiration whenever needed.

Animals are heterotrophs. They survive by eating the body parts of other organisms, using respiration to release energy from this food.

This hummingbird is using a lot of energy to hover as it feeds. Its muscle cells have thousands of mitochondria to release the energy they need.

Jan Ingenhousz
1730–1799

Photosynthesis was discovered by Jan Ingenhousz in 1779. At this time, scientists were only just beginning to understand that air was filled with different gases, such as oxygen and carbon dioxide. They also knew that plants gave out these gases in different conditions. Ingenhousz showed that oxygen is made only when a plant is in sunlight.

HALL OF FAME

DID YOU KNOW? Before photosynthesis evolved around 3.5 billion years ago, there was no oxygen in the air. In fact, oxygen was poisonous to most living things back then.

Plants in Extreme Habitats

Plants need light, water, and nutrients. There are many habitats across the world where these things are in short supply, but some plants have evolved special body parts and strategies to survive in these extreme habitats.

Dry Conditions

Desert plants spend most of the year waiting for rain. When rain does fall, the water trickles rapidly through the loose soil of sand and stones. The roots of desert plants spread out sideways, making a net that collects water from a wide area. After rain, desert plants begin to flower and produce seeds before the land dries out again. The seeds will lie in the dry soil and germinate during the next wet season.

Living stones from the deserts of southern Africa are plants with just two fleshy leaves that look like pebbles.

Conifer leaves are shaped like needles. This keeps the leaves from being damaged in winter.

Cold and Dark

Cold places can be just as dry as deserts because all the liquid water is frozen into solid ice. The winters in cold parts of the world are also long and dark. So, the plants that live there, such as conifer trees, grow only during the short summer when the ice melts. Since there is no time for conifers to grow fresh leaves in spring, the trees are evergreen, meaning they keep their leaves all year round.

HALL OF FAME

Sylvia Edlund
1945—2014

Sylvia Edlund was a botanist who spent many years studying Arctic plants. The habitat in the Arctic is tundra, where most of the soil is permanently frozen all year round. Only the top layer melts in summer, allowing small plants to sprout for a few weeks. Edlund discovered areas of lush plants in hidden tundra valleys that were fed by the water from melting snow.

Cacti are common desert plants. They have thick stems and branches with fleshy interiors that help store water. Cacti are green because all parts of the plants are able to photosynthesize.

A large cactus has a deep root that will reach down to damp soils far underground.

The leaves of this cactus are not obvious. They grow as sharp spines. The spines protect the plant from animal predators.

DID YOU KNOW? Welwitschia are plants that grow in southern Africa. They have only two leaves that can reach 13 ft. (4 m) long. These plants can live for more than 2,000 years.

Animalia

There are around 10 million species of animals that make up the kingdom Animalia. Members of this kingdom range from myxozoans that can be seen only under a microscope to large sea creatures in the oceans. The Animalia kingdom is split between 35 different phylums, based on shared characteristics between the creatures.

Tissues and Organs

Tissues are made up of animal cells that combine to perform specific functions. These tissues make up muscles for movement and nerves for sending messages throughout the body. Together, different types of tissues form organs that help animals break down energy, breathe in oxygen, and circulate blood throughout the body.

Kangaroos have powerful hind legs. Their muscles allow them to leap great distances.

Cellular Respiration

Animals eat plants and other animals for energy. Their digestive systems help absorb nutrients from food and break down the carbohydrates, fats, and proteins within it. Once broken down, these substances enter the bloodstream. Cellular respiration further transforms them into storable energy called adenosine triphosphate.

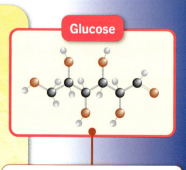

Glucose

The carbohydrate glucose is the main source of energy for animals. It is broken down in the mitochondria of cells. Excess amounts are stored in muscles or the liver.

HALL OF FAME

Carl Linnaeus
1707–1778

Carl Linnaeus named the Animalia kingdom in 1758. He classified animals into six groups: mammals, birds, amphibians, fish, insects, and other invertebrates. Linnaeus did not have an understanding of evolution and instead grouped animals based on their appearance, but his work laid the foundations for the modern classification system scientists use to identify new species today.

Blue whales eat a lot. The mammals are able to swallow more than 16 tn. (15 t) of prey daily.

These animals make calls that can be heard from hundreds of miles away. They can be louder than an airplane's engine!

DID YOU KNOW? Glass sponges are believed to have the longest lifespans in the kingdom Animalia. Some live for more than 10,000 years!

Animal Cells

An animal cell has no cell wall, just a flexible outer cell membrane. As a result, these cells have no distinct shape and take many forms. Like plant cells, animal cells have several types of internal structures called organelles.

The skin is also called the epidermis. Epidermal cells are dead, dried out, and able to form calluses. Trumpet players often get calluses on their lips.

- Nucleus
- Golgi apparatus
- Mitochondria
- Cell membrane
- Endoplasmic reticulum

The cell membrane has pores and pumps in it that allow materials to enter and leave the cell.

Inside the Cell

An animal cell contains several kinds of organelles within its cytoplasm. The nucleus stores the cell's genetic information and determines what the cell does. The mitochondria produce energy. A folded membrane called the endoplasmic reticulum is where the cell makes its useful chemicals, and the Golgi apparatus transports materials.

Specialization

Animal bodies are made up of many cells that work together. Each type of cell is specialized to perform a certain job. Sponges are one of the simplest kinds of animals, with just four cell types involved in processes that allow for feeding and reproduction. There are more than 200 different types of cells in a human body. All human cells contain the basic set of organelles, but some have developed other features, such as flagella or cilia.

Sponges are filter feeders that draw water in though their funnel-shaped bodies.

DID YOU KNOW? A bird's egg is a single cell. The ostrich egg, at 5 in. (13 cm) long, is the biggest animal cell in the world.

HALL OF FAME

Camillo Golgi
1843–1926

Microbiologist Camillo Golgi made many discoveries about animal cells, especially in regard to the shape and structure of nerve cells. The Golgi apparatus, an organelle in every complex cell, is named after him. He first discovered small traces of this organelle in the 1890s, but it was not fully described until the 1950s.

The soft lining of the cheeks is covered in a loose layer of cells. These can be collected easily and viewed under a microscope.

This nucleus shows up well, but smaller organelles are harder to see without a more powerful electron microscope.

21

Simple Invertebrates

Invertebrates are animals with no backbone or hard skeleton inside their bodies. They make up around 97 percent of all animals. Invertebrates come in a great variety of shapes and sizes. The simplest of all are sponges, which form funnel-shaped bodies for filtering food from water. Other invertebrates include worms, jellyfish, and mollusks.

A sea slug is a kind of mollusk that has no shell. Other mollusks without shells include squids and octopuses.

Soft Bodies

Jellyfish belong to the phylum Cnidaria. These water-dwelling creatures are all soft-bodied animals with tentacles that have stinger cells capable of shooting poison darts into anything that touches them. In addition to jellyfish, this phylum includes corals and sea anemones. Unlike most animals, cnidarians do not have heads. Instead, their bodies are rounded with a mouth in the middle.

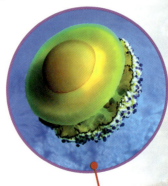

The fried egg jellyfish swims by squeezing its bell-shaped body, which pumps out jets of water.

HALL OF FAME

Hope Black
1919–2018

Hope Black was an Australian expert on mollusks. As a teenager, she started work at the National Museum of Victoria. Within 10 years, Black became the first woman to be made a national curator in Australia. In 1959, she joined one of the first female teams to explore Australia's Antarctic islands.

22

Mollusks

Mollusks form a large group of invertebrates. Many mollusks, such as snails and slugs, live on land, but most of them are aquatic animals. They often protect their bodies with shells. Snails have a single shell, while shellfish, such as clams and oysters, have two shells connected by a hinge.

A mollusk's shell is made mostly from a hard stonelike chemical called calcium carbonate. This shell protects the animal's body and keeps it moist.

The antennae on the head of a sea slug are used for detecting chemicals in the water.

A sea slug has bilateral body symmetry, meaning the right and left halves of its body are mirror images. There is a head at one end where the mouth, brain, and main sense organs are located. The other end has a rear opening for waste.

DID YOU KNOW? The geography cone shell is one of the most venomous animals in the world. Its venom is 10 times more powerful than a king cobra's!

Arthropods

The largest animal phylum is the invertebrate group Arthropoda. Its phylum name means jointed foot, referring to how these animals have an armorlike exoskeleton, or hard outer skeleton, made up of interlocking jointed sections. An arthropod's exoskeleton is made from a flexible plastic-like material called chitin. There are three main subgroups in this category: insects, arachnids, and crustaceans.

Insects

Insects are by far the largest group of arthropods. In fact, 80 percent of all animal species are insects. Insects have six legs and bodies in three sections, with a head, thorax, and abdomen. They often have one or two pairs of wings on the thorax. It is thought that insects were the first animals to evolve flight around 320 million years ago. Common kinds of insects include beetles, flies, ants, and butterflies.

The scarab has a tough cover protecting its wings.

Pill bugs are among the few crustaceans that live on land. However, they can survive only in moist habitats, such as among fallen leaves. Some species can roll up into a ball to fend off threats.

Crustaceans

Crustaceans have a varied number of legs, often with limb-like appendages that are used as pincers. Most of them live in the ocean. Copepods and krill—two types of crustaceans that live as plankton—are among the most numerous animals on Earth. Larger crustaceans, such as lobsters, toughen their exoskeletons with calcium carbonate. Other crustaceans include barnacles that glue themselves to rocks, filtering food from the water with their feathery legs.

DID YOU KNOW? Very few kinds of insects live in the ocean, with the major notable exception being sea skaters. All others live on land or in fresh water.

Arachnids have eight legs and limb-like mouthparts called palps. Most arachnids kill using venom. The venom turns their prey to mush, which the arachnid then slurps up.

A spider has two body sections. Its legs are attached to the forward section, called the cephalothorax. The rear section is the abdomen.

Spiders create a netlike web of sticky silk to snare prey. The arachnids use their feet to pick up any vibrations from movement in their webs.

HALL OF FAME

Margaret S. Collins
1922–1996

Margaret S. Collins started attending university at the age of 14. She became only the third Black American woman to become a doctor of zoology. Collins became an expert in termites—wood-eating insects that live in huge colonies and can damage houses made from wood. She was also a leading figure in the civil rights movement in Florida.

Lower Vertebrates

Vertebrates are animals with backbones and internal skeletons. All of today's vertebrates evolved from fish that first appeared around 500 million years ago. The first land vertebrates were amphibians—the ancestors of today's frogs and salamanders. From there, these land animals evolved into reptiles and the ancestors of mammals. Birds evolved later from dinosaurs.

> Amphibians spend the first stage of their lives in water, swimming around as fishlike tadpoles. They then grow legs, transforming into adults that move on land.

Reptiles

Reptiles have skin covered in tough, waterproof scales, and—unlike fish and amphibians—they are not reliant on water to breed. There are three major types: turtles and tortoises, crocodiles, and squamates. This last group is by far the largest, containing snakes and lizards. Most reptiles lay eggs with a waterproof shell, but a few give birth to live young. They are cold-blooded, meaning their bodies are the same temperature as their surroundings.

> Snakes have evolved to slither on their bellies without legs. There are about 4,000 species, and 600 of them use venom to kill prey.

HALL OF FAME

Bertha Lutz
1894–1976

Bertha Lutz became a leading expert in poison dart frogs. These brightly colored little amphibians collect poisons from the insects that they eat and store them in their waxy skin. Even touching these frogs can cause sickness or even death for predators, so animals learned over time not to attack the frogs. Two frog species and four lizards are named after her.

Fish gills are located behind the head. Water enters the mouth, flows through the gills, and then out through slits on the side of the neck.

Fish

There are 33,000 species of fish. They live in oceans, rivers, and lakes. Fish use gills to take oxygen from the water, although a few species can breathe air for short periods. They have streamlined bodies that flow easily through the water, and they use tail fins for swimming and side fins for steering. The back, or dorsal, fin stops them from rolling onto their sides as they swim.

The horned frog of South America has a mouth that is large enough to swallow prey that is the same size as the frog!

Adult frogs have no tails, while salamanders and newts keep their tails into adulthood. Amphibians return to water to breed. Their eggs have no shells and will dry out unless they are laid on or under the water.

DID YOU KNOW? The marine iguana is the only lizard to feed under the sea. It eats seaweed. When food is scarce, the lizard shrinks in size to save energy.

Birds

There are around 10,000 species of birds, most of which are capable of flight. Birds are vertebrates with two legs and a pair of wings. To take to the air, a bird's body must be both lightweight and strong. Flightless birds, such as ostriches and penguins, have adapted differently. Ostriches have swapped the ability to fly for large size and speed on land, while penguins use their wings as flippers while swimming.

> Birds have no teeth. Instead, their mouths are formed into a hard beak or bill. The shape of the beak indicates what food the bird eats. Hooked beaks are for ripping and cracking foods. Pointed beaks are suited for picking up small items, such as insects.

Primitive Birds

Birds evolved from dinosaurs around 150 million years ago. The descendants of these first birds are known as fowl. They include waterbirds, such as ducks and geese, as well as ground birds, such as chickens and partridges. Waterfowl are strong fliers that often make long migrations. The mute swan is one of the largest flying birds of all. However, ground birds spend most of their time feeding on the ground and are capable of only short fluttering flights to escape danger.

A partridge

A bird's wing shape shows how they fly. The rectangular wing of this eagle is ideal for soaring and slow, controlled flight. Smaller triangular wings are for faster flight with tighter turns.

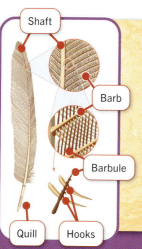

Shaft
Barb
Barbule
Quill   Hooks

Feathers

Dinosaurs were the first animals to have feathers. They used them for warmth. Birds do this, too. The feathers near their skin are small and fluffy, trapping a blanket of warm air. Feathers are made from keratin, the same material in mammal hair and reptile scales. Wing and tail feathers are flat and stiff because the many branches of keratin are neatly joined together.

Bird skeletons have no tail section. However, the animals create a tail with long feathers. This tail helps with flying. It is used for steering and braking. Some birds use their long tails to communicate.

Songbirds often have brightly colored feathers. This makes it easier for mates to find each other. Many birds often sing to show off their presence.

John James Audubon
1785–1851

John James Audubon is famous for making a record of all North American birds, including pictures of each species. He published his full set of images from 1827 to 1838, and they are still used to identify birds today. The National Audubon Society was set up in his name to protect birds in North America and across the world.

HALL OF FAME

DID YOU KNOW? The hooded pitohui from New Guinea is one of the world's only poisonous birds. It collects toxic chemicals from the ants it eats and stores them in its skin.

Mammals

The most varied and widespread vertebrates are mammals. All mammals have hairy bodies for at least some of their lives, and they feed on milk from their mothers' bodies when they are young. Mammals come in all shapes and sizes. The smallest are the size of a thumb, while the largest—the blue whale—is as long as two school buses. Mammals are warm-blooded, which means they maintain their own constant body temperature. As a result, mammals can survive everywhere from the icy polar seas and high mountains to steamy jungles and dry deserts.

Marine Mammals

Instead of legs for walking, mammals that live in water have flippers, which are much more useful for moving through liquid. The marine mammal group known as cetaceans includes dolphins and whales. Cetaceans have no legs and never come on land. On the other hand, pinnipeds, the group that includes seals and sea lions, come up on beaches to rest and are able to shuffle short distances on land.

Antelopes are hoofed mammals. These plant-eating mammals have long legs tipped with tough hooves, which are like very thick toenails. Long legs help most hoofed animals run fast.

Like all cetaceans, dolphins have smooth skin and nostril-like blowholes on the tops of their heads for breathing at the surface.

Hair is made from shafts of dead cells coated in keratin. It grows from a root embedded in the skin. Keratin is also used to make fingernails, claws, and hooves. Some animals have a keratin coat to make their skin waterproof.

DID YOU KNOW? The musk ox is the mammal with the longest hair. Some of its hairs grow to 40 in. (1 m) long. This long coat forms a thick barrier against the Arctic wind.

Marsupials

Most mammals are born after developing inside their mother's uterus. Female kangaroos and other marsupial mothers have small wombs, and their babies are born early in their development. The baby, or joey, then moves to a pouch on the mother's belly, where it drinks milk and continues to grow. Marsupials are mainly found in Australia, although there are marsupials in North America and South America, too.

Kangaroos do not walk. Instead, they hop along on large, bouncy back feet. This is an easy way to get around, especially when carrying a big joey in the pouch.

The cheetah is the fastest running animal. It can reach speeds of 68 miles per hour (110 kph) but only for a few seconds. The extreme effort makes the cat very hot, and it has to stop and cool down before continuing.

HALL OF FAME

Nikolaas Tinbergen
1907–1988

Nikolaas Tinbergen was one of the first scientists to study the ways animals behave in natural conditions. This field of study is called ethology. Tinbergen wanted to understand why animals acted the ways they did, especially those that lived in groups. In 1973, he won the Nobel prize for his work revealing why social groups succeeded.

Social Groups

Some animals spend most of their time by themselves, avoiding other members of their species. However, for other animals, it is common to gather into groups. There are many reasons for crowding together.

Chimpanzees live in troops made up of a mixture of relatives and friends. The apes are always competing to show dominance.

Herds and Flocks

Large animal groups provide safety in numbers. Some seabirds spend part of the year gathered in flocks on cliffs, hoofed animals form vast herds, and fish school in tight shoals. Predators that attack often have a hard time singling out one individual. A solitary animal would be at greater risk. Animals in groups also rely on their many sets of eyes to spot danger, warning others if a predator is nearby.

Gannets are seabirds that compete to nest in the middle of the colony, where it is safest.

Eusocial Animals

Ants, bees, and wasps are examples of eusocial animals, where a large colony of related animals work together to raise the young produced by just one member of the group. This organized social system is very good at keeping the colony alive during periods of drought or low food supply. Other eusocial species include termites that eat wood and naked mole rats that eat roots.

Leaf-cutter ants do not eat leaves but feed them to a fungus garden in the nest. Then, the ants eat the fungus.

DID YOU KNOW? Locusts form very large groups called swarms. One of the largest swarms ever recorded was spotted in 1954. It had around 10 billion insects.

Chimps communicate with calls and expressions.

Apes spend a lot of time grooming one another, cleaning dirt and insects from their fur. This helps to form social bonds.

HALL OF FAME

Jane Goodall
Born 1934

When she was 26 years old, Jane Goodall went to live alongside a group of chimpanzees in the forests of Tanzania. She watched how the apes behaved and communicated, and she built up a picture of how chimp societies worked. Goodall found that chimpanzees made simple tools to collect food. Ever since, she has been studying primates and fighting to protect animals and their natural environments.

Animal Bodies

Of the many millions of animal species, each one has evolved to live in a unique way in a specific habitat, which has led to huge diversity in animal shapes and sizes. One thing many animals have in common is a body that is capable of actively moving to gather food.

Fish have a skeleton made from bone and cartilage. This gives the animals their shapes.

Body Symmetry

Most animals have a bilateral body symmetry, which means that the left side of the body is a mirror image of the right. This bilateral plan is seen in everything from worms to whales. Bilateral animals have a head at one end, a waste opening at the other, and a distinct top and bottom. However, a few primitive animals, such as the sponges, have bodies with no head and no symmetry at all. Jellyfish, sea stars, and their relatives have radial symmetry.

A centipede's body is constructed from several repeating segments. Many animals have bodies organized like this, with different segments specialized for different tasks.

A snow monkey keeps warm during winter by taking baths in volcanic springs. Its fur also becomes much thicker but will thin out in warmer weather.

Frequent Changes

Animal bodies can change a lot throughout their life cycles. From insects to frogs, many animals have a larval phase. These young animals look very different from their adult selves and survive in a completely different way. For example, a caterpillar larva eats leaves while an adult butterfly sips nectar. Similarly, mammals and birds change seasonally. They develop thicker coats of hair or feathers in winter. Then, they shed them for a cooler covering in summer.

HALL OF FAME

Pierre Belon
1517–1564

Pierre Belon was one of the first scientists to study comparative anatomy. He compared the body structures of different animals, such as humans and birds, to look for differences and similarities. This process was an important step in understanding how animals—and all other kinds of life—are constantly evolving.

Sea anemones are named after a type of plant. Early biologists thought they were seaweeds, but sea anemones are actually meat-eating animals!

This sea anemone has no hard body parts. Instead, it has a hydrostatic skeleton made up of capsules of water. These capsules are flexible and can keep their shape, giving the anemone's muscles something to pull against.

DID YOU KNOW? The longest animal in the world is the siphonophore. These close cousins of jellyfish have tentacles up to 150 ft. (45 m) long.

Animal Locomotion

There are several forms of animal locomotion. The most primitive is swimming, which involves movements of the body to push an animal through water. Some animals, such as squid, propel themselves with jets of water. Walking, running, and climbing all make use of legs and feet, but many land animals get around without them.

> Moving by jumping is called saltation. Kangaroos are famous for getting around like this. They lean forward and raise their long tails to stay balanced in the air.

Air Time

Animal movement over land often involves spending time off the ground. When an animal is walking, at least one foot is on the ground at any time. While running, an animal's feet are off the ground for short leaps. Gliding is different from flying. It is a slow, controlled fall from a high starting point to a lower landing site. Expert gliders, such as sugar gliders, can stay in the air for several seconds.

> True flight is when wings create a force that allows animals to travel up away from the ground. Only four types of animals have evolved true flight: insects, bats, birds, and pterosaurs.

HALL OF FAME

Eadweard Muybridge
1830–1904

Eadweard Muybridge was a pioneer of moving images. He used many cameras set out in a line to take photographs in order. Together, they could be made into an early form of video. Muybridge used his system to capture the way animals, mostly horses, moved. His videos showed how the legs moved differently when the animal walked, trotted, and galloped.

Slithering

Snakes are an example of legless animals, but others include caterpillars, worms, and maggots. There are three main ways a legless animal slides. In rectilinear motion, the body ripples in an up-down wave as it slides forward. In the second method, the body loops from side to side as it pushes on the ground. The third method is sidewinding, in which wavelike body movements push the animal sideways instead of forward.

Sidewinding is useful for moving efficiently over loose desert sand.

Kangaroo forelimbs are free for holding food, cleaning fur, and boxing rivals!

Kangaroos are known as macropods, meaning big feet. The tendons connecting their feet to their leg muscles are very stretchy, so the animals bounce without having to use much energy.

DID YOU KNOW? Young spiders create sails of silk strands to catch the wind and take to the air. This traveling method is known as ballooning.

37

Animal Reproduction

The aim of life is not just to survive but also to reproduce and increase in number. Animals will divert their resources to reproduction, often going without food in order to succeed. Sexual reproduction is the most common method for animals, with each new individual having two parents. However, there are many different strategies to get the best results.

This aphid is giving birth to daughters using asexual reproduction. The baby insects have no father, only a mother. She can give birth very quickly without needing to find a mate.

Aiming for Quantity

Smaller animals often use their resources to produce large numbers of young. The females lay many small eggs, and the males fertilize the eggs after they are released. The parents have little ability to take care of large numbers of young, and many will die before they are able to breed themselves. However, this strategy allows just a few animals to rapidly populate a new habitat if that opportunity were to appear.

Frog spawn is left unguarded in the water. The eggs will hatch into tadpoles that must fend for themselves. Most will not make it to adulthood.

Aristotle
384–322 BCE

Animal reproduction was not fully understood until the early twentieth century, when the science of genetics and inheritance showed how DNA was passed from parents to offspring. Before this, people believed that small animals, such as worms and aphids, appeared spontaneously from rotting material. This idea came from Aristotle, a Greek philosopher who is considered to be one of the first biologists. He made detailed records of sea life in the waters near his home.

HALL OF FAME

Orangutans have the longest childhoods of wild animals. Mothers spend nine years raising each of their children.

Parental Care

An opposite reproductive strategy is to have only a few young at one time and invest time and resources into protecting them. This maximizes the chances of offspring reaching maturity and having a family of their own. The babies of animals that use this system are often born very helpless and require parents to carry them and find their food. Eventually, the offspring learn to do this for themselves.

All the baby aphids are genetically identical clones of their mother. As soon as they are born, the babies are already preparing to have their own offspring.

Asexual reproduction means that aphids can spread fast, covering a plant in just a few days.

DID YOU KNOW? Each year, an oceanic sunfish produces 300 million eggs. Often, only one or two of these offspring will reach full adulthood.

Other Senses

Some animals have different senses that appear to give them superpowers compared with how humans experience the world. Snakes can see prey from the glow of their body heat. Sharks can find hidden prey from the electric pulses they give out. Meanwhile, bats can navigate their way in the dark using sounds.

Heat Sensors

Several types of snakes, most notably pit vipers, have patches of heat-sensitive skin on their snouts. Heat rays, also called infrared radiation, give a kind of invisible light that human eyes cannot detect. Human skin can feel heat, which helps people avoid fires or stay out of the sun. However, the vipers' pits are able to detect the body heat of prey in the dark.

Pit viper venom is slow-acting, so prey often runs off after a bite. The viper follows, keeping track of its meal using heat sensors.

This shark, like many aquatic animals, has lateral line sensors. These sensors run down the sides of the body and are highly sensitive to water motion flowing past them. Lateral lines detect the water currents made by other fish swimming nearby.

Echolocation

Bats hunt mostly at night. Many catch small flying insects in midair. Most animals would need very large eyes to spot tiny prey, especially in the dark. But big eyes would be too heavy for bats. Instead, bats give out high-pitched calls that echo off their surroundings. The bats pick up the echoes with their large ears, using them to figure out what is around them in the dark.

A bat's call is so loud that it closes up its own ears to avoid damage. Then, its ears open again to listen for echoes.

HALL OF FAME

Marcello Malpighi
1628–1694

Marcello Malpighi was one of the first scientists to use a microscope for investigating how animals worked. He discovered important features about the kidneys, lungs, and blood vessels. Malpighi was also the first person to see the electroreceptors on a shark's snout. These sensors, called the ampullae of Lorenzini, are named after Stefano Lorenzini, who gave a more detailed description.

The hammerhead shark's flat snout is covered in gel-filled holes that pick up the small electrical fields created by the bodies of other animals. The wide head allows the shark to quickly find prey, even if these creatures are buried in the sand.

The mantis shrimp is able to detect 12 colors of light—compared with the human limit of 3. The animal can even spot ultraviolet light, which is invisible to humans.

The shark's skin has tiny toothlike spikes that allow it to slice through the water.

DID YOU KNOW? Two-thirds of a shark's brain is devoted to processing smell. It can pick up blood in the water from 440 yards (400 m) away.

More to Explore

Each year, scientists discover thousands of new plant and animal species. They estimate that more than 80 percent of land species and 90 percent of underwater species have yet to be identified. Scientists expect to find many more species of plants and animals in deep ocean waters, tropical rainforests, and remote mountainous regions as they continue to explore and research.

Amphibious Mouse

In 2022, an amphibious mouse was discovered in the Amazon Rainforest. This particular mouse has partly webbed feet and feasts mainly on aquatic insects. According to scientists, the newly discovered mouse belongs to a rare group of semi-aquatic rodents.

Medicine

Many medicines found in pharmacies are made from plants. These include aspirin, morphine, and many cancer-fighting drugs. So, the potential discovery of new plant species is especially exciting. These finds may prove useful for medical purposes.

For thousands of years, people have used plant-based medicines. Ancient writings suggest that plants were used as early as 3000 BCE.

Scientists recently discovered several new species of insects in India and the Philippines that use camouflage to make themselves look like leaves. These creatures are often called leaf insects or walking leaves.

Human Species

A possible new species of humans was recently discovered. The *Homo juluensis* species lived in eastern Asia around 300,000 years ago. A group of researchers from the University of Hawaii made this amazing discovery from fossils originally found in northern and central China. While creating a new organizational system for fossils, they happened to find similarities between jaw and teeth fossils found in different sites.

Review and Reflect

Now that you've read about plant and animal biology, let's review what you've learned. Use the following questions to reflect on your newfound knowledge and integrate it with what you already knew.

Check for Understanding

1. What are eukaryotes? What are taxons? *(See pp. 4-5)*

2. What process do plants use to power their bodies? How does this process work? *(See pp. 6-7)*

3. Name and describe three structures of a plant cell. *(See pp. 8-9)*

4. What parts of a plant are used in photosynthesis? What do these parts do? *(See pp. 10-11)*

5. Define pollination and germination. *(See pp. 12-13)*

6. Explain how both plants and animals get their energy. *(See pp. 14-15)*

7. How are plants in the desert different from plants in very cold places? How do both of these compare with plants in less extreme habitats? *(See pp. 16-17)*

8. Describe the process of cellular respiration. *(See pp. 18-19)*

9. Name and describe three structures of an animal cell. *(See pp. 20-21)*

10. What are some differences among different kinds of invertebrates? *(See pp. 22-23)*

11. Name and describe the three groups of arthropods. *(See pp. 24-25)*

12. In what order do scientists think vertebrates evolved? *(See pp. 26-27)*

13. Give at least three reasons why animals gather in groups. *(See pp. 32-33)*

14. Name five methods of animal locomotion. *(See pp. 36-37)*

15. List three senses that humans don't have but other animals do. *(See pp. 40-41)*

Making Connections

1. What are some similarities and differences between plant cells and animal cells?

2. Choose two living things described in this book to compare and contrast.

3. Choose two people mentioned in the Hall of Fame sidebars who studied similar topics. How might the work of one have influenced the work of the other?

4. In what ways does an environment affect how plants and animals evolve and live?

5. In what ways are vertebrates and invertebrates alike and how are they different?

In Your Own Words

1. Choose a person described in the Hall of Fame sidebars. How is this person's work relevant to what we now know about plants or animals?

2. This text mentions the wide biodiversity of living things in the world. How do you think living things might benefit from biodiversity?

3. Imagine you gained one of the senses or abilities mentioned in this book that is usually unique to plants or non-human animals. How would having that sense or ability make your life different?

4. Scientists continue to study plants and animals. What areas do you think they should focus on? Why?

5. Which fact in this book did you find most fascinating and why?

Glossary

bacteria a large group of single-celled microorganisms, some of which cause diseases

biodiverse full of many different kinds of plants and animals

carbohydrate a substance containing carbon, hydrogen, and oxygen, such as a sugar or starch

carbon dioxide a waste gas produced by the body, made up of one carbon atom bonded to two oxygen atoms

cell the basic unit of plants, animals, fungi, and microorganisms

cellulose a substance that is the chief part of the cell walls of plants and is used in making products, such as paper and rayon

chlorophyll a chemical that green plants use to help make their food

DNA short for deoxyribonucleic acid, the chemical ingredient that forms genes

invertebrates animals without a backbone

membrane a thin, flexible layer of tissue around organs or cells

metabolism the chemical processes that the body's cells use to produce energy from food, to get rid of waste, or to heal themselves

molecules small units made up of two or more atoms

nucleus the central part of a eukaryotic cell, which controls its function and stores its DNA

organ a group of tissues that work together to do a specific job

organelles parts of cells that do a job

organism a living thing, such as a plant, animal, fungus, or single-celled life-form

photosynthesis the process of plants using sunlight to create sugars out of water and carbon dioxide

pollination the transfer of pollen so that plants can reproduce

predators animals that feed on other animals

respiration the metabolic process that releases energy from sugars

species a group of similar-looking organisms that can reproduce

tissue a collection of cells that look the same and have a similar job in a body

vertebrates animals with a backbone

Read More

Kallen, Stuart A. *Climate Change Impact: Ecosystems (Climate Change Impact).* San Diego, CA: ReferencePoint Press, Inc., 2025.

Kroe, Kathryn. *What Are Fungi and Molds? (Germs and Disease).* New York: Cavendish Square Publishing, 2023.

Martin, Claudia. *Marine Ecosystems (Ocean Life).* Minneapolis: Bearport Publishing Company, 2025.

Miller, Verity. *Inside Biological Taxonomy (Inside Modern Genetics).* New York: Rosen Publishing, 2022.

Learn More Online

1. Go to **FactSurfer.com** or scan the QR code below.
2. Enter "**Plant Animal Biology**" into the search box.
3. Click on the cover of this book to see a list of websites.

Index

amphibians 19, 26–27, 42

arachnids 24–25

arthropods 24

bacteria 4, 8, 13–14

birds 15, 19–20, 26, 28–29, 32, 34–36

bones 22, 26, 34

brain 23, 41

carbohydrates 8, 18

carbon dioxide 6, 10, 14–15

cellulose 8

chimpanzees 31–33

chloroplasts 8, 10, 14

crustaceans 24

cytoplasm 8, 20

deoxyribonucleic acid (DNA) 8, 38

development 12, 20, 31, 34

echolocation 40

egg 12, 20, 22, 26–27, 38–39

feathers 28–29, 34

fish 19, 26–27, 32, 34, 40

flight 24, 28, 36

flowers 6, 12–13, 16

forests 11, 31

frogs 26–27, 34, 38

fruit 12

germination 13, 16

glucose 8, 14, 18

habitats 6, 16–17, 24, 34, 38

insects 11–12, 19, 24–26, 28, 32, 34, 36, 38, 40, 42–43

invertebrates 19, 22–24

jellyfish 22, 34–35

leaves 6–7, 10, 13, 16–17, 24, 32, 34, 43

locomotion 36

mammals 19, 26, 28, 30–31, 34

marsupials 31

microscopes 9, 18, 21, 41

mitochondria 14–15, 18, 20

mollusks 22–23

nucleus 4, 8, 20–21

organelles 20–21

oxygen 14–15, 18, 27

photosynthesis 6–8, 10, 13–15, 17

pollen 12–13

reptiles 26, 28

respiration 14–15, 18

roots 6–7, 10–11, 13, 16–17, 30, 32

seeds 6, 12–13, 16

sharks 40–41

snakes 26, 37, 40

social groups 32–33

species 4–6, 18–19, 24, 26–29, 32, 34, 42–43

spiders 25, 37

trees 6–7, 9–16

vertebrates 26, 28, 30

water 6–8, 10–14, 16–18, 20, 22–24, 26–27, 30, 35–36, 38, 40–41

48